Perihelion
Poetry Collection

Roberta Batorsky

© Roberta Batorsky
Published by Prolific Pulse Press LLC
Raleigh, North Carolina USA
October 2025

ProlificPulse.com
admin@prolificpulse.com

ISBN: 978-1-962374-60-6 Paperback
ISBN: 978-1-962374-61-3 ePub
Library of Congress Control Number: 2025918819

Cover & interior Art Design by KRynae Design Co.

Dedication

I want to thank Rodney Richards, Elliott M Rubin and Doug Stuber and members of their writing groups for their collaborative insight, good humor, and mentoring. And Kirsten Johnson for patiently reading the manuscript.

I dedicate this book to my husband Carl, my children Rebecca and Ben, grandchildren Felix and Oscar and to my mom for provoking me to write.

Table of Contents

Acknowledgements

Poets Sing Happy Poems Anthology, by Rodney Richards, "You Are All I Need," "Shoulder Your Burden" and "Pashtun Sanwich"

Social Possibilities, "Pashtun Sanwich"

NJ Bards, "Unbooked, A Year Without Reading"

Heron Clan, "Tremolo," "Dry Goods and Their Discontents," "Perihelion"

Poets Write Science, "Chimera"

I went to the doctor

He said, "You got a hole in your head,
that's making you manic.
Get back to basics;
eat only organic."

Sprung me out of asylum
dosed with Clonopin and Xanax.
My priest said I need religion,
so I tried to find myself in Islam.

Then, close to complete collapse
my mental health in pieces,
I gave myself to Jesus,
afraid to have a relapse
or worse, wind up in prison.

Almost free of substance
save the occasional indulgence,
I'm vaxxed up, living healthy,
avoiding notoriety,
jazzed on open mic poetry.

American Standard *or* The Loo's Lament

From the smallest room in the house,
save the outhouse,
I object strenuously
to my new destiny in the dump.

My porcelain ellipse now awaits
being hacked apart by a sledgehammer.

After loyal service for over 30 years
you replace me with a trendy,
quiet, one-piece, low-flush model.
Your only excuse:

Gotta protect the environment

Hasn't my sturdy rim held
your semi-comatose form after a binge?

I've given you emotional and physical support
        been completely receptive
                discreet about your excesses
                plunged, suctioned
                smeared with excrement
        turned a blind oval to all jokes at my expense
        seen you at your least flattering
        had snakes driven through me

AND WHAT FOR?

To be overlooked for a trim, chic,
whiter, unproven model?

It makes my water level surge.
Evidently, loyalty isn't enough.
Consider this while I flush one final time.

The Night They Burned Old Angie's Down

Angie's Mexican Luncheonette
boasted tongue-searing chili,
crispy tacos and bursting burritos
until one October night
when it was incinerated
to the last smoking timber.

Crushed flatter than a tamale,
wisps of charred chorizo
hung in the air,
the frijoles refritos doubly refrito,
ropa vieja more vieja than ropa.

We await with mucho anticipation
a rekindled Angie's;
to bring our hambre to be stroked
by salsa nuzzled
nachos embraced
enchiladas stuffed
con sabor Mexicano.

Social Dancing on Neptoon*

Ballroom dancers
Arthur and Katherine Murray,
commanded the dance floor,
classic examples of suaveness and grace,
effortlessly, stylishly, gliding
as one elegant body.

They box-stepped, twirled,
waltzed and cha-cha'ed
into our living rooms,
inspiring Mom as a sure way
to cure her pimply, plump
teenager's perceived unpopularity,
improve her self-image,
and, in Mr. Murray's words,
put a little fun in her life.

I agreed to dance lessons
at a local studio.
Since partnering with Mr. Murray
was out of the question,
I surrendered myself to the arms of
the male part of the class,
short, dark and sleazy,
in tight pants, shirts unbuttoned
to their hairless breastbones.

They, one after the other,
pressed themselves
hard into me,
their brilliantined hair
brushing my nose,
hot, steamy breath
in my cleavage,
our legs entangled
with each reverse turn.

My social dancing future
dimmed with each crisp heel pivot
and cha
cha
cha.

*Neptune Ave. Brooklyn

Robot Queen Machine
For Deb, 6 years after her death

What did they mean
when they formed us?
Did they mean us to be lean
or something in between?
Did they mean us to be keen?
Is it OK to be green
and not easily seen,
or something in between?

When they formed us
what did they really mean?
Pop and Mom together,
plainly to be seen.
Or, was a stranger in between?

Did they plan us being actors
on the silver screen?
displayed, heard, and seen,
provocatively mean,
or something in between?

Children of our parents
we display their hybrid sheen.
Leaving home before I fledged
myself barely a teen.
That was pretty mean!

After 50 years in treatment
still asking relentlessly,
what did they really mean?
Will I ever be serene
or, something in between?

Mom's bawdy rhymes and verses
purty near obscene.
The poetess laundreate
of the degenerate, hipster scene.
What did she really mean?

What did they really mean
by putting us in between
and not letting us be seen?
No one tried to intervene.

What did they really mean
when they formed us?
Did they mean us to be clean?
Or something in between?

Lost Lives Matter

After my grandson puts out the skulls, dragons, bats,
spiders, bones, and gaping coffins, he asks
Did you ever touch a dead body?

I bite my tongue,
as not to crush
his joy for the coming holiday
with my adult grasp of death.
Can't shrug off the mantle of my years.

The memory of Mom,
lifeless under a still warm sheet;
she, gently and finally,
was placed into a bag and
removed on a stretcher.

I was a witness for Dad,
kissed a cold cheek,
stiff skin clings to bone,
expressionless death mask
scarier than any lawn decoration,
or eerily carved pumpkin,
lit from within.

I carried their ashes of grief,
later poured them on living water.
No store-bought silken shroud could
evoke such a sense of dread.

Enjoy your treats.
Set your kooky ghouls in the yard.

Your lives will soon include losses
costumes and candy can't chase away.
I try to live down
my sad ghosts, lost lives,
new tenants of the island
between now and then.

The ear still hears for brief moments after death.
I love you; we are with you.
Safe journey.

Flat, but Festive

There's a hand-crafted matzah called shmurah
Coveted by some students of Torah
Which, given no time to rise
is bread in a novel guise

Save your gelt through the year
buy it when Passover is near
It's not found in your 'hood
just the Lower East Side
B'klyn or Lakewood.

If you hold focaccia and ciabatta dear
and your bagel with a smear
this holiday at the very least
you must cut down on your yeast

You plunk down forty shekels
even though that price seems high
to have your shmurah
approved of by a rabbi.

For this consecrating rabbi
capping the water is paramount
he's demanding, some say crabby
That's right; keeps a strict account

From your choice of Passover Matzah
of which you will find lotsa
the one I prefer,
the most *pareve* for me,
shmurah is also sold gluten-free

Irreplaceable, *for Marianna (RIP)*

Older sister, fine violinist,
caring teacher,
lives in her car,
alone.

Think,
how to help her

The strings take up the melody,
her bow drawn against them,
sorrowful strain,
chord   sustain,
vibration hangs   midair,
silence   follows.

Unstrung, for Richard
Cue the string section

His aristocratic, page-turning fingers
advance the music, hesitate,
finally falter.
The stand partner, by his side,
displeased,
rejoins the orchestra slightly late
at the next measure.

This awful disease,
muscles spasm
out-of-control, destroys
all pleasure in playing,
substitutes its own staticky
discordance
for his impeccable
sense of rhythm,
coarsens his fine intonation.

His toes cramp
when his feet clock the timing,
twitchy legs skip a beat,
eyes wander,
lose his place in the score.

The conductor's gaze meets his:
something wrong there?

Hands loosed on the neck,
the viola clatters to the floor.
He swipes at it,
to no avail
fearing he'll soon follow.

Playing was everything to him.

ritardando
slow the music
  to a halt
    let it
      all
      go.

The orchestra resumes
the final movement,
strings now thinner
by one good player.
diminuendo, then

Finale.

I Remember It

Your solidness and righteousness:
used like a packhorse in your work,
broad back arched with weight.
Sinews broke sweat under a load,
you resigned to it.

Mornings early wakening
inured to routine,
sleepwalker craved sleep's surrender
you revived in it.

The scars from a fallen crate
your torn scalp, black-stitched head
raised horror in me,
unsettling your placid features.
You laughed, not angry, puzzled,
you relished it.

Forged of defective clay, blistered,
torn unformed from home,
trusting nobody,
you relived it.

Weighing the world's wrongs
against your unkind treatment,
clear-eyed, not vengeful,
you reconciled to it.

I think deeply on your sadness,
forgiveness, endurance,
give you the respect held back
while you lived.
I regret it

Your sudden death sundered me,
I hold your scars within me,
cradle them with tender love.
I remember it.

Poverty of metaphor

These things remind me of you
but don't summon you:
the tides ebbing and flowing,
changeable moon
showing its lovely phases,
footfalls echoing on pristine snow.

and they, as you,
won't appear
in this poem.

Metaphors of ancient rivers,
mountains endlessly climbing,
waterfalls cascading,
don't conjure the complex
emotions I feel for you,

absent, as you are,
from this verse.

We roamed graceful hillsides
made promises, broke them,
said tearful farewell to family,
ecstatically welcomed births.
Our years now measure twenty.

These snapshots,
tarnished surrogates for you,
will not be included
in this or any poem.

The poem:
how your head tilts to me,
shoulder supports me,
footsteps forever follow.
These are the *objects* of life,
not the *subjects* of verse,

and, like you,
won't be mentioned
in this poem.

Love

With rod and tape,
hourglass, stopwatch, and all
I weigh the world with you.
But wisely you scorn
the bulk and weight
as level and probe
chart the slide from plenty
to numb and hollow.

Drain the sidewalk cracks
of our tears-
fill the rain barrel to overflow-
our faces in the filmy drops
dissolve,
leave oily smears.

Heart muscles shudder,
chambers unfill,
shunt the portion of love
to memory,
the ebb and reversal
bring extinction.

What I know:
hurt deadens love.
The hourglass
you leave behind
is drained and wanting.

Me and Iris under the boardwalk

Taking a long pull on the glass mouthpiece,
Iris passes the pipe to me,
dark ashes collect on the white sand
under the boardwalk.

Two crumpled forms huddle close,
faces silhouetted in the flickering
glow of smoldering hash,
vacantly peer between the slats
up at the clear night sky.

We're sprawled here
since school day's end for me.
Iris, graduated in June
trawls for work in the morning
armed with a secretarial degree
shorthand, typing, dictation,
picks me up at 3 on
days I'm not truant
in Mrs. L's rusty old Rambler.

When I have better things than school
to do and no soul home to account to
we scamper to Gerritsen Beach
prowl the dunes,
hide in the beach grass,
laze on the abandoned jetties,
dangle feet in the murky water,
laugh at our wavy reflections.

Other days
we head to Brighton Beach boardwalk,
nestle beneath its plank walkway
'til sundown when Iris unveils her
glass pipe and fires up the contraband.

Tall, skinny with flame-red hair
she lives in the "projects" with her mom,
won't attend college, suppose I won't too.
Her boyfriend writes long letters
from boot camp, Fort Dix.

Moist from her tears,
she reads them aloud,
wrinkled by countless unfolding.
Her ankle boasts a tattoo:
a red flame inked with 4U below.

Wish I was you
brave and cocky,
had pierced ears like yours

Mom hates you so completely
banned you, called the cops
said you stole from her
and you laughed.

What future in store?
your example charts a way
no problem for you,
singing Spoonful's
Summer in the City,
under the boardwalk.

Song of the Shorebird

The shorebird's guttural call
is for mating, display
and territoriality,
to ward off competition.

In some species, both sexes vocalize.
The dunes give protection
to plovers, terns and young 'uns
exposed and open,
lives like yours and mine.

After leaving the nest,
before they fly,
they still need care from predation.
The sky is full of dangerous objects.

The foghorn blasts to shore;
the sleeping gulls scatter,
downy and perfused in lyric light,
settling in for a rough night.

Without boundaries,
where the heart breaks

I wait for you.

If I die first

Breaking into the crystal silence of noon
your scan shows bones and nodes
absent free range cells with their noxious cargo,
tumor contained.

My heart echo captures
normal rhythms,
vessels shouldering
their muscular burden.

The years bring
an increase of diagnoses, some transient,
others solid,
translucent raindrops
on the windowpane,
fuse in wavelets.

I fret the shifts, collect changes,
age-launched,
bemoan the relentless,
ticking clock that

if I die first
leaves you lonely.

Excuse me

My student asked for extra time
to hand in her assignment.
This lament I have heard
more than once,
patience isn't my strong suit.
Forbearance is given
with a reasonable explanation
and meekness of attitude;
a dominance-submission
game I find tedious.

The student explained
she was a witness in court and unasked,
slid down her oversized shirt
revealing blistered,
angry scars covering
her bare upper arm,
a sorry vision burnt
everlasting into my memory.

Flinching, tears in my eyes,
I managed to stammer
I'm sorry
please cover yourself.
How can I help?

From then on,
hardship extensions were permitted
for the flimsiest of excuses,
understanding offered,
no questions asked.

My New Identity

The Star of David flag long ago
swelled my breast
                    for the last time
Cover my head
Fast for my sins

The Shofar speaks
God's voice to his chosen people
Obey commandments
Marry in the tribe
                    no more
Child of my father
Plant trees for the dead
without understanding
it wasn't empty land
                    It's over,
                    over and done
Gone in the desert winds
                    Trust is broken
Respect my elders
Keep holidays and Yahrzeit
Mourn every loss
of one or a million as my own

Raised to discount
disavow, disrespect
our common humanity
binding us to this earth,
my heart changes itself,
rejecting customs, politics, and bias:

I embrace my new identity.

Picking Apples in Stilettos

Memories on Mom's death:
Not her fractured hip,
cancer diagnosis, or when
she spouted gibberish
expecting we'd understand:
the cancer was talking.

It's her unselfconscious humor,
cartoonish looks,
Bozo the clown hair,
overdone make-up,
when she dug out her car
from a snow pile
in flip flops with a spatula,
picked apples in stilettos,
shoplifted small and large items
beneath her bulging coat,
squeezed into size zero jeans,
drove her convertible
top down in winter,
wrote jingles for every occasion,
put mayonnaise in everything,
read me Dorothy Parker,
brought me salty chickens on the subway
when I was pregnant,
kept her dampened ironing in the refrigerator,
chain smoked,
drove drunk,
set the kitchen on fire,
offered the firefighters a "hot toddy"
lied when she could be caught,
cooked matzoh brei,
slept naked,

sung show tunes off key,
stayed out nights,
hid chocolate bars with the linens,
suntanned relentlessly "to look healthy."

No novelist could invent this concoction
of narcissism and childishness.
Nurturing, inspiring, sacrificing, empathizing,
all traits consistent
with mothering,
were not in evidence
to my best recollection.

Bismillah

I palm the cheese wheel
warm from the udder it squirts from.
Bismillah
before the slaughter of ovines,
asks blessings and forgiveness for the
lamb flesh in the sack,
caressed in my arms.

Humbly I thank
the giver of this bounty:
the cracked wheat jostling
preserved lemons,
oil, yogurt, figs, olives
and grape leaves.

The butcher:
Where have you been all year?
Teardrops at my cheek,
a catch in the throat.

First shop visit in a year,
nourishing, gesturing, welcoming me
to resume my life.
Bismallah

Death Shall Have No Dominion

from Dylan Thomas

I refuse to be complicit
in the presence of death.
Even complacency
is controversial,
not just on this continent.

It's pretty complicated.

Collecting my thoughts:
at some point,
the living and dead
will converge
in a colossal convocation,
but I can't be convinced
without more context.

Conceptually,
this can cause a commotion,
even a crisis,
which concerns me
in no small way.

Carefully contemplate the consequences.

Teen Troll

My lipstick-streaked lips purse,
press against Mom's mirror,
I proudly survey the
caked residue that clings to the glass,
blood-red stained teeth decorate my smile.
My reflection of a teen's garish gaze
turns me on, like Mom's
sultry succubus.

She honed her hold on the male sex,
delighting in the envy of her own.

From early hours
she slopped on makeup,
concealed a face nice enough
without pots of pancake powder,
daubed-on liners, glosses and rouge.

None of it reduced her years,
or restored to her the youth
that coursed through my own veins.
She couldn't recapture that by design.

My quick study of her moves
and methods rewarded me
with a married boyfriend
twice my age, rendezvous,
instead of school,
copying her example.

I find myself much, much later,
wear my furrows, freckles, and lines,
mementos of the years,
don't wish it were otherwise.

A knowing face grins back at me.

The Child Lighter

The soft squeak could be a late winter nuthatch,
deflating balloon, kitten purring,
coming from deep inside my chest,
its silken rhythms follow each of my exhales
the dark echo sometimes wakes me.

What's that?
Do we have mice?

Breathing deep can't quell my worry
or still the rumble in my lungs.

A butt, always dangling from Mom's lips,
waggled up and down when she spoke,
plumes of smoke sometimes tracing an ellipse.
Embers from butts stubbed into
deeply-stained ashtrays glow
in dark rooms,
acrid smells linger on surfaces.

The penalty passes to a grown child
whose untried lips hold
the smoke stick.

Immature but capable
nine-year-old's hands press,
hold down the igniter,
sees the spark, then flame,
of the special Bic lighter
brings it to her face,
before placing the lit ciggie
in Mom's accepting mouth,
beginning the day.

Sine qua non*
for my poetry group

Love of every kind
so eloquently described here
is perfectly mapped
onto its coordinates

Old love   saves
the most tender of embraces
for declining, ailing bodies
Young love   pushes
up against the barn
in daring, puppyish play
Same-sex love   tastes
thirsty lips with
a shudder of delight
Loyal love   serves
her coffee in morning light
as children sleep
Titillating love   regrets
near misses,
                    dreams
of pendant breasts
and indiscretion

All of it love,
in endless variety
given abundantly,
without which nothing

It's all in the poems.

*means without which nothing

New Year to Be Born

the year 2022
my 2 weeks in a locked ward on 5 psych meds
no visitors or cell phones senses dull - blank
unfeelable

my paranoid roomie checks under bed
screams all night hears voices

across the hall from us
a beautiful mom of teen-aged twins
the ward alert sounds her self-harm
bandaged arms, dosed with ECT

our beds -
thin lumpy mattresses on a plank
no springs
weapon risk
regulation only 2 coverlets
no shoelaces or ties on clothing
self-harm risk
hairbrushes confiscated
no bottles of anything even water
drug risk

emphatic, positive words mandate normalcy
drug-free recovery
sobriety cover the walls
also food stains
bathroom door absent
no shower curtain
leaky windows barred
escape risk

outside my room where I can't go
three elegant does and

a tiny spindle-legged fawn appended to one
                                                    lingers
ELOPEMENT DANGER
KEEP DOOR LOCKED

affirmation classes during the day
would you care to share
spew lethal doses of prayer and gratitude on us
staff with forced saccharine smiles
leave promptly exit clangs shut

racks of partially filled-in
coloring books - one blank page
screams out--- please help me

new early morning admission

man strapped to gurney
face under a hoodie contorts with pain

someone moved my food
we're suspect
I try to instill calm but no avail when he re-emerges

straight-jacketed not to be left alone with us
anymore
food uneaten

blood draws at 5 am
tas-t cakes all flat and crumbling
gravy indiscriminately blankets everything on a plate
fried chicken or beef bourguignonne

only spoons for mealtimes
assault risk
I can't eat anything - weight drops daily might need
ensure

walking all night then morning meds
night nurse reads Norse sagas
spies me prowling 'til dawn
room doors left ajar
hall light intense no shaded corners

me: poor judgement confusion unaware of
surroundings
stay or go same to me
many lifetimes elapsed 'til now
meds tapering to zero- I cook dinner
see
know
wish
want
write
am
     myself
                a

          world

Natick Anew

Walking the city streets
I walked thirty years ago,
knowing that every street
walked the last time
elicits imagery,
feelings of loss and separation
like now.

The years haven't changed
my love of space,
my breath as it was then,
friends
  children
    running
      laughing
        dancing
          hugging
            crying
all *tossed* in the air
          landing   where?

I have a sense of all of us
some names forgotten,
countless children, now grown
frozen in time,
cast in a swirling glitter-globe
off-center
twirling through this recovered space,
breathing into it
inhaling the chill air
of the New England fall.

Cut, Print

Cary Grant and Loretta Young,
in *The Bishop's Wife*,
asked the director to film
only their left profiles
to capture to best advantage
their fan magazine looks
on celluloid:
impossible to do in the same shot

Sam Goldwyn said
if I only use
half your faces
in my blockbuster
in return you get half pay,
which offer was politely declined.

Herein a filmic metaphor for relationships:
You need to allow
the effect of your good
as well as bad sides
to reap full benefit
and allow your co-star
their share of the limelight.

Life imitates art

Pull Aim Squeeze Sweep

My partner's hand clasps my shoulder hard.
We move apace
towards the raging fire pit,
matched steps crunching on gravel.

Visibility down, our eyes tear,
faces bead with sweat
in the oppressive heat.
The fire's deafening roar
obliterates other noises.

We near the licking, teasing blaze,
gloved hands grip the handles,
remove metal pins on the flame squelchers.

In some future scenario
could we assist in a burning building,
rescue a trapped child,
smother a wildfire intent on destruction?

With a steady, purposeful arc of an arm
the compressed gas exits
Pull Aim Squeeze Sweep
leaving smoldering plumes and ash
where an inferno had raged.

Clackety-clank on the rusty truck bed
as we discard the spent cylinders
with team spirit and *joie d' vivre*
clamber alongside.

Past the 'jaws-of-life' cars
boasting scars of shattered windshields
and accordion-pleated doors
hanging off bent chassis for demonstration.

The training ends:
We twist tourniquets over fake blood vessels,
bandage imaginary scalp wounds,
carry to safety dummy victims
planted in a dark, obstacle-strewn room
in jerry-rigged chairs.

BRI, Fat Rebranded

The gauge of obesity, BMI,
recently under scrutiny,
is being slowly ousted
by a new stat using geometry
in place of weight and height.

Scientists and physicians
decided BMI wasn't alright.

JAMA* says body rounding index**
is more accurate,
a more complex surrogate
to measure fat deposits.
A BMI under 25 is ideal
but at or above 30,
health issues are revealed.

BMI ignores the weight that's fat,
where it lays,
in this BMI falls flat.
'cause it downplays
muscle, bones, organs, and water
(it shouldn't oughta.)

Why is BRI a better stat?

Adding height, waist, and hip inches,
the healthy zone is 2.3;
anywhere higher or lower
is not where you wanna be.

Old people, less jacked,
with more fat, rank leaner than in reality.
Their BMI, minimized with age,
hides any abnormality.

Health risks are downplayed
with only weight and height.
Scientists agree it just ain't right
and give BRI a better grade.

*Journal of the American Medical Association
**BRI

The Lonely Traveler
For Benjamin

Spilled out over the planet
you tread open spaces
cities hushed by night
busyness tramps past
not yours
odd language roughens the ear
beyond your ken

boy
unclaimed

Quit this solitude
submit to it
plunk seed down
so it grows

boy
you imbibed my strength
took home in my breast
to proffer a birth
not yours
not alone

Stroll empty streets
surveys of detachment
forlorn temples stand for longing
lonely traveler
when all looking stops
will seeing begin

boy
still unclaimed

Soul Sister-In-Law

Sandy saw sounds.
slumbered fitfully,
waking suddenly and soundlessly,
somewhat surprised.

Her art was her life.
Her look all her own,
How many days I missed her,
since my divorce.

Sandy heard smells.
Comfortable with her beauty,
relaxed in her skin,
never sanctimonious.

Sandy painted in rhyme,
Bob Marley, superstar's
Revolution Song.
Rebellion suffused her build.

How many times I missed her,
strong in her beliefs,
creative artist,
sisterly-wise and street-smart.

Serendipity surrounding,
Sandy blew kisses
to me through the window
smearing seamlessly.

Try to show tenderness
in life lived without her.
Simulate the semblance of smiles
for yourself.
Sandy tasted sights,
somewhat sarcastic but
consumed by sadness.
Never simple.

Life without her is serious,
sleepwalking without symmetry.
She sang songs
echoing in my head.
Finding her in this poem,
her wide brown eyes
and midnight black hair,
shining softly.

When I first spied her,
standing aloof,
forgetting, not forgiving
and hardly ever fidgeting.

It took me thirty years
to build life without her.
Sandy was solemnly scared of sickness.

In loving her,
I am alone with memories,
of her strangeness,
simultaneously sinister and soothing.

What You Bring

For Carl

Meat in the stove for the dog
partially paralyzed, deaf, poor sight,
dog needs carried.

Mom in extended care
also deaf, can't walk,
recognize herself,
watches tv with vacant eyes
spoon fed by aide.
weekly visits
a task,
a trial,
a heartbreak.

You, violinist, strings unbowed,
unplucked,
fingers suddenly stiff, still,
off the bridge.

Eyes scanning for notes
that deserted their staff,
instrument at a remove,
decelerando,
absent accompaniment,
silent.

Surely, you'll play again,
rehabilitate,
bring back the music,
strings vibrate,
sweet sonorities,
allegro vivace

means life to you.

Tremolo
For Bliss Michelson (died from COVID-19 2022)

The quartet now
in high register
mourns its bottom end:
Strings so bereft, unstrung!

The *f* clef lives
below the bottom staff
where Bliss bows on:
The upright and so righteous
Bliss:
profound, deep in note
and cadence
is gone.

Low, the vibration
sweet, the sound;
soprano alto tenor bass.

The resolution:
the coda ends the movement:

Finale

The Remedy

Along with
the in-and-out breathing,
visions of wavy, petaled fingers
curling over seraphic skin,
broken, seeping,
betraying me as ever.

Interiors picked over,
revisiting night sighs past again,
leaving me: foolish, lonely,

miss me once,

miss me twice,

empty hulls
vainly waiting for deliverance.

Here's a remedy-
practice patience for an unfolding dream,
wake up when a chance of stillness
beams an interlude of solace-

the remedy.

Anniversary Poem

True love can't be measured by
the cubit, dram, or spoonful.
No vector determines its magnitude or direction.

Times and trials unspool themselves
when two hearts anneal to each other
binding there the right justice of collaboration.

The downy albatross
majestic against the horizon mates for life.

Two broken hearts find themselves
belonging beyond the scope of our vision.

These learn to wait for understanding
'til the learning sets like Jello in a pan.

To know another
syncing the weft and warp of times and trials

To know what to expect,
in unison to play the heartstrings.

We know how to wait and will.

The Dead Daughter

Mom never lacked ersatz Robertas,
her pals and substitute daughters,
I envied their intimacy.

They went out smoking,
drinking,
karaoke,
gambling, racetrack and parlor,
spilled confidences,
had hair and make-up dates.

They loved fast cars,
boxing,
flattery,
deceit schemes,
gossiping and
haute cuisine.

My Mom, thirty years their senior,
cultivated, kept them close, shared rumors:
me being a Weatherman
I can't live down.

Michelle, one of the Robertas, and
husband Hal
rode Harleys until
he was badly injured,
she killed
in a horrific highway accident.

We attended the raucous,
memorable funeral.
The cortège was headed by
fifty monster bikes,
bikers in full road regalia,
garish warpaint,
engines roaring.

We sped through lights,
honking furiously
amidst the clamor,
fearing for our lives;
bikers held up
the opposing traffic.

Never forgotten,
the tragic death of a
beautiful young wife and mother.

Horseflesh

I memorized women's bodies
not from an anatomy tome,
dressing room,
furtive glances at near-naked relatives
or mom as usual *en deshabille*,
my tour began in Loehmann's intimate
musty, try-on room.

At impressionable stages in my life,
Mom schlepped me along with
female relations to Loehmann's
where, in the fitting room,
was auditioned an unending array of
ill-fitting duds, garish get-ups,
and Muumuus.

Sally, Doris, and Midge
paraded in these togs to
elicit clucks of approval,
but more likely vigorous gagging sounds.

In the large, mirrored room,
reflections amplified pendulous breasts and droopy
behinds
forced with breath-held effort
into seam-busted Donna Karan,
Chanel, Goldworm, and Bonnie Cashin,
size four sample suits
featuring pencil skirts,
puffy shoulder pads
and peaked lapels.

Mom sniggered at the apparitions,
in size 2 Jordache jeans
she fit perfectly, if snugly,
into each costume
garnering "oohs" and "aahs" from
her envious audience.

Tall for my age,
my forehead
reached just chest-high
on the women.

I tried hard to avert my eyes,
but became a quick learner of
the contours, curves, fault lines
and outlines of the female form,

wondering how time,
use, abuse, and hormones
would sculpt my sapling shape.

Gloucester Beach

We clambered the rocky coastline
of Gloucester Beach,
in view of the commanding
Eastern Point Lighthouse and Cape Ann.

For years, its light guided lost mariners
to safety past ancient shipwrecks
into Inner Harbor.

From my craggy purchase,
I spied a man not fully in his own skin.
A familiar form awash in need,
flailing, unmoored against the skyline.

Each scaled boulder sent us further
from security of shoreline,
from sight of each other.

The worn, sharp-edged, uneven boulders
supported me against the bleaker weather,
my marriage in disarray,
the final painful sharing, none sparing.

The steepest incline afforded
no surface for grasping, ending my ascent.
The downhill was far trickier, less assured.

We moved hesitantly towards one another
on the slippery shoal,
knowing tomorrow would never be the same.

My Two Dinas

Dina 1 was a bottle-blonde.
Dina 2 sported Shirley Temple curlicues.
D1 tall in stilettos, gym-toned thighs
emerging shapely from a micro skirt.
D2 in worn-out Keds,
paint-spattered army surplus on her elfin frame.

D1 college student, took money for sex.
affected a cigarette holder
feigned Photoplay glamour
had manicures in chic salons
paid taxis to school on an expense account
made sparkling cocktails
with teeny parasols from her mini bar.

D2 sculptor and painter, trailed ashes behind.
Chapped, nicotine-stained fingers
always in motion, clay caked her nail beds,
made colorful sundials with
village kids under her wing,
didn't own a watch, slurped cowboy coffee
and hitchhiked with a simple sign reading "upstate."

D1 bemoaned life; the upkeep
of her image more demanding with age,
and the boozy, loveless encounters.

D2's life fueled her art as art animated life.
For her, change was possibility.

Thirty years later, I reconnected with D2 and her
wife at the Catskills gallery that embodied their flair
and imagination,
my best Dina.

Smaller Than a Fingernail

A tiny, stray seed springs
from my hope,
implants in me
amid the weeds and sand.

Nourished by tears and blood,
you force my vessels
to detour past you,
my diaphragm resists your kicks,
as you grow to fit
your velvet hollow home.

Once we melded,
shared smell, taste and warmth
until birth's privilege of breath,
space and time;
now the distance between us
is infinite.

Imagine you still move in me
and from that tenancy
garner support and strength
to grow and live
until you find every love you need

and quit the search.

To My Cousin on Her Ex's Death

Once you loved him;
he is gone to you and the children.
Your love ended years ago,
still your legacy remains.

Separation, divorce peel away love.
The tiniest flicker continues,
'til death snuffs it.

Now your heart space swells,
burgeons with
fond and fierce memories,
his face framed
in your children's features
expressions, gestures.

You hug them and feel
his pressure,
presence,
absence.

You start to say,

Do you remember when....?

to hear him laugh,
hold his sides the way he did,
but words freeze, unspoken.

What comfort is there
for a double loss?

How can a heart break twice?

Vertigo

Is the room dissolving or is it just me
Is it sepulchral gloom or thrilling fantasy
Am I facing up or down
Is this speed or stasis

What is this swarm of locusts in my head
Will I outlast them

Alls I know is:
When I walk it fake me
Where I look it fake me

Whippoorwill

Chants its name in Eastern forests
Senses a soul departing and captures it
Repeat

Whip-poor-will
Sounds like it, too

Even now,
sensing souls departing,
like me, reading the newspaper.

Cryptic night bird
Hear, not see, them.
Carries off souls

Whip-poor-will
Sounds like it, too

Soundier than 'nightjar,'
midsummer bird.

Even now,
like me, reading the newspaper.

Unit 4

The rear of psychiatric unit 4
abuts a close-cropped, treeless lawn.
Standing here,
I often glimpse a delicate doe
with her new fawn
envy them their liberty
even as mine, I relinquish.

I make the circuit
from the locked, bolted, entry
with "ELOPEMENT RISK"
in bold type, feeling empty.

Not caring to merely languish
I struggle with anguish.

Circumnavigating the nurses desk
to the rear window and reverse transit
I, best estimate, lap 100 a day,
avoid the workshops,
otherwise well-attended,
troubled souls being mended.

Three daily meals and two snacks
I happily avail myself of.
The latter, lack in variety consist, unimaginatively,
of overripe apples or packages
of stale Frito-Lay.

Eight days after admission,
discharged, optimistically,
in transition to a new suite of meds,
real or imagined suicidal ideations shed,
left in my vacant bed.
Gratis modern psychopharmacology,
I escape the grim specter
of ECT.

Birds of the Forest Floor

Drill beneath the canopy to see
carrion-eaters clear the understory.
Thankless job for
hawks, vultures, ravens, crows:
never unemployed!

The ungainly clean-head hoppers'
small-eyed, blinkless stares pierce,
rend, unearth, scrounge the darkness,
debride wounds of the dying, dead.

Hesitate to judge the forest owlet's
borrowed nest of carcasses' decaying flesh:
Cleansers take abandoned nests.

Nourish those who nourish you,
that nourish the forest
to make it capable and fertile
if it may be done.
if may be born,
if life could reinvent
and not ruin
as has done me.

For the buzzard, quick of eye,
find in its stare, kindness of a mother,
even sacrifice.
Sharp beaks and talons gripping
and me,
hard gripping back
in the unslept night.

What no one wants to see-
the recyclers make-fit:
the silky, lush-needled undersoil.

Ten Year Anniversary

to Rebecca and Luca

To my children and grands
cosseted in my breast:
you open my heart,
stir the best of me.

Ten years have passed
since two parallel lines fused,
charted new spaces,
tiny constellations,
congealed
formed
named
built
returned to the cosmos the life
which to them was freely given.

Two minor planets
escaped from fleeting time in synchrony

As our weary sun incubates coming days,
its heat sears the skin.

These additions say your names
reflect your builds,
wear your threads,
speak your verses.

Midday of the following day
my own years approach end,
time's sparkles paint out my shadow,
the breadth, beauty and depth of your characters
give me peace.

Chimera[1]

Pregnant mom's brain is mosaicked
by her nine-month tenant's
shed corpuscles.
Junior's cells home to her
Glands
Brain
Skin
Blood
Marrow

Thinking, eating for two
literally, in miscarriage too,
the varmints linger,
impose their wills.

A match in her body:
of fetal cell chess moves,
mom countering.

These runts squeeze
through placenta,
push mom's mammaries
to make more milk
suiting themselves,
turn up the heat
from thyroid gland driver's seat,
sashay into a sibling carried later
or even form tumors
with dire result.

Just another critter
staking out its territory
in the all-consuming
land-grab of birth.

[1] A chimera is a person with cells of two different genotypes, in this case, those of the mother and fetus.

Therapy Eclipse

Slowly the shadow ascends to the coveted place
to cross, block, conceal my therapy embrace

At the eclipse maximum irrevocable time is still
I'm denied entry, sun beclouded still

the penumbra barely illuminates
a bitter and misaligned pill

A Bad Year is Ending

This unfortunate year
drew us closer together
skirting misfortune in some ways,
travailing through in others,
partners in all weathers.

The body makes itself known,
we encounter barriers with increasing age,
illnesses and other maladies
some we are prone to.
We push them back,
shed tears of rage.

Your cancer narrow escape
caught us completely off-guard.
Your courage earns my admiration,
dearest to my heart,
I toast you in celebration.

Races and competitions
lost were formerly won.

Each goal met, less ambitious than before
at thirty, forty, fifty and on.
It's so difficult to measure,
feel satisfaction, even pleasure
when it seems you've just begun.

Good-bye to this uneven year.
Still, I am attracted, compelled,
to continue the life we share.
Two separate hearts bind as one,
together, forever held.

Autumn Finds Me

The hot summer stripped me bare
wrung me out, parchment-skinned,
sandpaper hide faded by glare.

Fall dips the mercury
jazzes my mood
with eager anticipation.
Feels like January.

Autumn finds us,
tots hiss past on bikes and scooters.
Kids in the street
abandon phones and computers.

Autumn enjoys its weather,
communicates delight as
breezes arc the trees.
It's early September,
pumpkin lattes brewed to please.

Moon chases sundown by seven,
New England clime.
Apples near to picking,
close-by Halloween time;
clocks are switching.

Autumn finds us as
our seasons collect,
shiny apples ripe on the branch.

Together in all weather,
neighbor to perfect,
not ready for the ranch.

Dry Goods and Their Discontents: Ballad of the Fitted Sheet

This is my complaint:
I am never folded correctly
because it's a two-person job.
My corner elastics are worn from washing.
I never get taken to the beach,
prop up a turkey feast
or other joyous family celebrations.

I am slept on at nighttime,
sandwiched between my flat partner and the mattress,
and, after laundering, take more room in the linen closet.
Deposits of mucus, earwax, semen, and menstrual blood
stain me even after bleaching.
I never go on a picnic,
am crafted into a curtain or
a hobo-bag.

Anchored to the mattress,
treated with carcinogenic flame-retardant,
and thrown out before my partner or made into rags.
The iconic image of a billowing sheet
on a clothesline never is me.

My round corners ball up and hoard
washcloths, hankies, panties
and at worst, single socks,
the latter now orphans,
found only after their mates
are landfills or recycling.

Ikea replaced my flat, life-partner
with a foreign sounding, suspicious,
less comfortable, Duvet-cover
and I am bereft.

Fishmonger

for Lisa

My great aunt Francis
never smelled from the slimy fish
she hacked apart.
Skillfully wielding her cleaver,
cleaning and deboning
for her loyal Lower East Side customers,
she displayed the red gills
Very fresh from the sea,
carefully wrapping purchases
in brown paper.

She washed her red hands in the tin sink,
scales clogging the drain,
before accepting payment
sometimes in coin.

She used to peddle her wares from a pushcart,
then moved up to a tiny Rivington Street shop.
Her short silver hair lay in a natural wave,
framed the sturdy face
and steely blue eyes
of a hardworking woman.

I remember
on one of my visits with my grandma,
Aunt Francis cutting open a fish,
exposing another small fish inside its body.
I think I remember this.

My limited understanding
at that young age
saw as an unborn baby fish
what was more likely prey.
In her walk-up tenement apartment.
my grandma and Francis had tea,
gabbed around the kitchen table:
family business and other boring stuff;
I was invisible.

My great uncle Yush rumbled in
from I didn't know where.
Some factory or hauling job,
signaled us to beat it
back on the subway to Brooklyn.
Me ducking under the wooden turnstile,
even then too old to do that.

I found out after she died
her given name was Leah.
Some Sylvias became Sally,
Polinas became Patty,
Basyas became Barbara.
Much later I found out my
mom Debra was Esther.

They all moved far away
from the Williamsburg Bridge;
Francis' store became
an after-hours jazz dive.

And the Debras, Barbaras
and Pattys, with new nose jobs,
moved far from Delancey
to Long Island or New Jersey,
eating store-bought frozen fish.

Shoulder Your Burden

It's not yours to shrug off.

Our solar system's sun, with resignation,
abandons mission and position.

And once rested,
begins a new day,
doesn't need convincing.

Shoulder your burden,
given the grace to which you were born.

Overturn insincerity, decry falsehood,
repel force with persuasion
and the knowledge gained over a lifetime.

Earth's magnetic force
exerts strength to protect us
from strong solar winds
without inducement.

Shoulder your burden
defy pretense
bring conviction and belief
to what you do.

Accept the struggle,
counter platitudes with truth and persistence.

Bring along wit and empathy
for good measure
to light your way.

<pre>
                    My
    Dis   connect

    I rope   you sand
    I burlap   you water
    I belay   you fumble
    I sundial   you smog
    I rudder   you tides
    I savings   you scam
    I precision   you seepage
    I dry   you cascade
    I anvil   you tears
    I spine   you nosebleed
</pre>

Lose this number

My Shift on the Hotline

people phone the hotline in
desperate straits
some I identify with
others, don't go there
I offer empathy and referrals,
putting them off
you think.

can't change their lot
or offer an anodyne
disrespected
abandoned
despairing
depressed
homeless
pregnant
hungry
shamed
pained
robbed
       alone

how can I help you?
sounds hollow, sterile,
dismissive to me

their characters and complaints
populate my brain
as they, anonymously,
struggle to live their lives,
support families, quell distress,
stay erect,
sensing a confidant,
briefly, in me.

then I hang up and move on

Drinking with Mom

Night comes, not drowsy,
homework can wait.
I grab a highball glass,
Slurp slowly my J and B.

This private time with her is special,
a captive child audience,
up post bedtime,
laughing at late-night TV.

We watch weird people's headshots,
sound muted,
she laments her lot,
boozily assigns to others blame for her life.

I hear things I can't understand,
feel privileged by her confidence
until our ruckus rouses dad.

He shouts, anguished,
Why are you keeping her up
She has school.

Mom and I exchange secret smiles,
suppress laughter at him, agitated,
foolish, exposed in his boxers,

We bond in this comic interlude.

Morning unfolds,
he lumbers back to bed
his disapproval
heavy in the room.

Perihelion

The corkscrew tendril hugs the branch
teaching tenacity to spiky seed arils sunk in snow
and blind nightcrawlers
deep-burrowed in streams of translucent pebbles.

A largo of forgetting
builds to a wintry cadenza
while cardinals roost in dense evergreens,
force solitary strands of communion
through the latticework of time.

Decide which notes to mute or sustain
for better or worse
Your choice to make:
to people this pilotless planet.

Camera eyes envision a sand dune
with the semblance of snow in a glitter globe
where a photograph of a photograph in a locket
holds a memory tethered by a single hair.

My Pink Leg

Five digits wink up at me,
protrude from soft white gauze
below a hard hot pink cocoon.
My ankle and shin kept rigid
below a knee and thigh moving freely,

the two body parts
can't collaborate to
convince an uncooperative foot,
stuck ankle to initiate a stride,
limiting me to a helpless hobble.

This disaster resulted
from failure to overstep
the hidden branch
and a messy fall:
balance betrayed.

My misgiving:
does this avoidable misstep,
the dropped beat,
reveal age's imperfections,
distractions, betrayals
and can recovery restore agility?

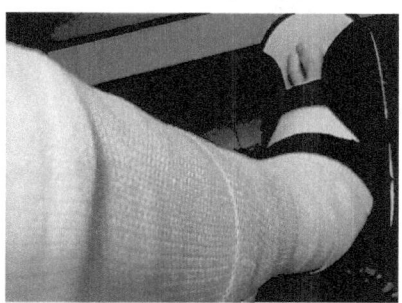

Man to Man

Been working out?
How's your dead lift?
I benched one fifty
Been on night shift

Put an add-on to the garage
Playroom for the twins
Did you catch the playoffs?
Best of seven wins

New microbrewery in town
Let's go, my dime
Ditch the girls on a pretext
When I get done overtime

You say you wake up to pee?
They check your prostate?
You may need a biopsy?
You know me, I'd wait

I rototilled the back plot
Tossed in a few seeds
Homegrown tomatoes
worth pulling weeds

Let's plunk in the canoe
Grab your tackle gear and line
We'll troll for brook trout
Come rain or shine

What background noise, you ask?
my toilet, you hear   or
the better-half trumpeting
my day's tasks, *coming dear*

ZOOM

Heads to each other
we are
a perfect array
in disarray.

We meet in a dream of life
defying death
surrounded.
Disordered, distanced possibilities,
an impossibility.

Random, atonal music,
ascending descending
percussive invasive.

Heads to each other
dissolving kisses in finite embraces,
infinite embraces.

Runway to Nowhere

did you visit
was I home
can't place the face
you say is me

recognition in
            free
                fall
halting sounds
blank conversations
hellos   goodbyes
some shouted
lips move   no content

what I hear:
fragments   dissonant
can be   painful
what I see:
staticky screens
blurry features
neither you
nor me
nor us

you
hope   memories linger
to bring me comfort
peer at me through a veneer of habit

the body occupies space
as unclaimed baggage
spins on a carousel

who are you
why do you say these things
should I know you
can you leave now? I need rest

You Are All I Need

Not knowing where love stops
or begins
I bury myself in you
for my hungering heart knows only
a hangdog winter.

I rush to you
with surfeit or loss,
emotions loosened
in your warming breast.

Neither art nor device
can lift this dread off me.
You are all I need
to signal my new season
and nudge this frozen shell
back to life.

With you I am the hidden spring
or the shaded stalk
hesitantly blooming
where new growth stirs,
shudders
and sprouts.

Sorrow yields to opportunity
to announce the looming spring
and love extends its righteous span,
sighs, grows to overflow.

The Racing Turn

The undulating nymph
swinging or somersaulting
signals the ear.
Move the endolymph

If you think your life lacks vim and vigor
is pretty banal
sensors detect xyz movement-
crystal displacement-
in your semicircular canals

Gymnasts and divers
Forward roll
How droll
       Inversion
             Perversion
                  Balance askew
                        Nausea

Un-remember

I remember your life better than you:
alone after school, four kids
watch tv through a neighbor's window,
eat government-issued cheese,
lose your dad,
mom's family burns up in Germany.

Not my own life,
still, the pathos and joy of it claim me.

Your mom parents me better than mine.
Aunts, uncles, cousins around us,
children, some ours, play everywhere.
Love around us,
surrounds us.

Your personality costs us:
friends become enemies,
lost to us.
You, so *sure* how it should be,
claim to know, decide for me,
'til I push back, get hit for payback
bring in police.

The female cop you call "girl":
This girl packs a loaded weapon.

I paid for my freedom to start again.
If only I can un-remember your life,
to claim my own.

In Loco Parentis

The dedicated crossing guard,
a yellow cross emblazoned across
his jacket
name unknown to us,
in rain or shine
stopped traffic,
bodily, when necessary,
mouthing "STOP"
with a smile,
arm upraised

Only to descend
after children's boots
navigated the busy
intersection,
safely meeting the opposite curb.

One day,
a speeder took him out.

Children and parents
lost a protector.

In memoriam, local hero.

Flowers blocked
his empty post for weeks,
disabling the intersection.

Invocation

May buzzards peck your liver
Flies nest in your eyes
Your blood thicken and clot
Worms plug your airway
Your skin glistens and oozes

As your bones crumble into ash
May fires sour your churning guts
Wild palsies grip your hands
River rats gobble your tongue
Tremors rack your limbs
Cureless diseases enfeeble and pain you

Forever your warped vision disables you
As you know no season save winter
As happiness goes uncharted
Children won't remember you
Spirit unrested
Your heart busted with sorrow as mine.

My Lunar Addiction

My hands stab at the moon's
complacent orb,
encircle that pale, swollen globe.

How humbling,
not star or planet,
entrained, as am I,
into the yoke of orbit.

I swallow its dimpled fruit
ingest, replace
the relentless throbbing in my chest
with the even, deliberate cycling
of belonging.

My heart pounds, pulse soars
nerves shatter
in ramping up, taking down
my dependence:
the phases repeat,
me mounting a hopeless response.

Insomnia, a wildflower
fragrant as to defy
the need to rest.

I keep vigil even
as the moon's pull draws
part of earth in tides,
hope for calm
in its waning crescent.

Tod

The man seated by the therapist
points to his legs held stiffly before him.
When his turn to speak to our group,
reveals in soft tones
that his baggy sweatpants
cover recent third-degree burns.

He intones as if to himself,
These are self-inflicted.
He punctuates his halting speech
with awkward giggles
although his face belies tragedy, not humor.

I'm so ashamed.
I didn't want my kids to feel I did this to them.
I had to get away from myself.
I am so ashamed.

He continues irrelevantly,
Only one man was perfect, and he was crucified.

The dim light streams in from the window
casts his face in partial shadow,
reveals his hands resting atop one another,
trying unsuccessfully to suppress a tremor.

Their constant movement, paradoxically,
draws our attention.
Two wings of a trapped insect;
the top hand prevents its partner
from launching around the room,
finds a corner in which to alight,
momentarily quells his agitation.

He has difficulty staying in one position,

seated upon a pillow, shifts weight
from one buttock to the other, pain evident,
clears his throat frequently
preliminary to speech but fails to begin a
conversation,
instead shrugs his shoulders with a sigh.

The thin voice gains strength when the topic
isn't himself: The rotten weather, work,
unsuccessful attempts to meet other singles.

I avoid his gaze, try not to stare at his legs.
But I need to know: *Is the skin peeling?*
How far do his burns extend?

Hearing about his self-harm
gives me anxiety mixed with empathy,
not shame or condemnation.
Instead, sorrow for whatever version
of the human condition
caused his need to self-destruct.

Like a phase of the moon a crescent shadow flits
across his face, brows furrow, corners of his mouth
turn down, a shudder runs through his body.

I don't blame you
Can you find peace?
an affirmation for your wounding self?
re-examine your life for meaning
reverse this inward turning? find in the moment
reason to live?

Now the starry sky's dark eminence
yields its blackness to a blanketing sunrise.
In my imagination I cradle his wounds
to offer a reason to continue another day.

An Apple a Day

A magnificent Marin County day
for a teen's cycle jaunt
a short ride to a favorite haunt
until an SUV in the way
rams the child, sends him into
the passenger side

The driver yanks free
the blacked-out guy
beats a hasty retreat
no attempt to notify-a failed deceit

Teen's air pod stuck
under the mat
points the authorities
where the van is at

The phone's "Find My" app
tracks the driver who sped from
the scene of the crash,
formerly-at-large
now felony charged

**Air pod solves crime
speeder does time**

Thank-You Card

for Deb

It don't fit
I read it
Have two already
You spent money on this
Tastes spoiled
We are off carbs
Not my color
My husband's allergic
No room for it
Out of style
There's a smell
Not sure how to use it
Didn't I gift you this
Can't you use it
I don't iron anymore
PLAID!
Would you donate it
Keep the receipt

Thanks, I am sooooo grateful, Deb

Soup Dumpling

For Xue

Hard to describe this wonderful treat
Yummy so good to eat
A Chinese source of national pride
Is it soup or a dumpling, you decide

Be careful don't pierce it
Leave the casing unsplit
Slurp it, suck it, I'll be your guide
Is it soup or a dumpling, you decide

Catch the drips with a spoon
If it opens too soon
Two worlds here collide
Soup or a dumpling, you decide

Slice it open so softly
Eat it with green tea
Down your gullet it glides
Find something wonderful inside
Soup or dumpling, you decide

Anyway, It's Home

We live at the intersection
of Hinkle Drive and Hinkle Drive.
Which is to say, our abode abides
in the Hinkle crosshairs.
With affection, Hinkle Crossing.

Since the appellation Hinkle
is also awarded a court, terrace, and street,
One wonders
I do anyway

Who was Hinkle to deserve
such honorifics bestowed upon him.
Did he even know?
What were his/her/its pronouns?

Our Hinkle nest is deposited
smackdab in the middle of
the Charles Bossert development
of high ranch and split-level postwar
homes which since sprouted
cupolas, bump-outs, garage conversions,
dormers, sunrooms, decks, patios,
circular driveways, mudrooms and solar.

I don't know what a mudroom or a bump-out is.

All testaments to creativity
of the home-dwellers
and the accretion of prices since the 'fifties.
The Charles Bossert/Hinkle
designations give rise
to a further query:

What was the relationship,
between H and C B
the former with no first name and binomial Charles?

Does having namesake two drives,
and one each terrace, street and
court convey less stature than
a namesake development?

It should be noted that when denizens
of Bossert refer to Bossert
other Bosserters and even Hinkletonians
know whereof they speak.

Charlie Chaplin's Great Dictator
was Adenoid Hynkle,
not Adenoid Bossert,
less mirth giving.

Thomas Paine, Clara Barton and
Napoleon's brother Louis
all former residents of Bordentown
(who was Borden?)
in which Bossert lies made the informed choice
to reside in Bordentown City
not township:
lower-class, Republican-voting.

The regional school district
comprises students from city and township.
The city with nary a Hinkle.

This configuration of the city or borough
and township comprising
a regional school district
is peculiar to New Jersey.

Past Acrost Pasta
For Dolly with thanks

Not eaten yet
Why they feed us?
      Eggplant parm in a dish
They knew she was lush?
      Broccoli rabe sauced on a plate
Out with lover?
      Pasta with pesto
In car crash again?
      Gnocchi with red sauce
Family at dinner acrost alley
Shop 'til she dropped?
Forgot who she is?
Found a new bar?
      Lasagne en casserole
Left us for good?
      Ravioli Bolognese
Faces at window
Empty plates sent back with no *thanks*
      Cannoli, powdered sugar

When a heart breaks, feed it

The Walkers in the Rain

Debora sets the pace;
we circumnavigate the quad
our voices shrill, disconsolate,
muffled by summer rain.

No one eavesdrops on us.
Background and language divide,
wounds rivet us, briefly, together.

Mary peels the damage done:
Shawn destroyed our house,
punched in the walls,
hit me in front of my kids.

Debora tolls the damage done:
Four years ago, Steve destroyed my car
with me inside.

Roberta yells the damage done:
Poking, pinching, spitting, biting.
Can't hide from the anger
not above the law
or behind the rain.

Of a breath we sprint for the canopy,
where six children suddenly appear,
a rainbow in an oil slick.
This vision shrinking into anonymity,
wanes too.

We mothers in sad union
born of pain and betrayal,
voices cadenced, walkers in the rain.

Sea Glass

In lockstep we trample past the long blades
of slimy bull kelp that litter the black sands,
where ancient inky rock was pummeled to gravel.

The spreading dune grasses give shelter
as coastal twilight descends on us.
furtive
ominous

We find frosted sea glass
transformed, pitted, roughed in the tides
weathered edges smoothed, tumbled,
ground relentlessly eons ago
slick, slippery, translucent.

Tomorrow's tide's retreat
will reveal the extent and shadow of your deceit –

    our rental you paid with cash,
    c-notes you mailed for plane fare
    your phone calls while I slept

will sweep to shore
an empty picture frame
that held your family.

The sea lions wail your betrayal.

Grasses protect the fragile dunes
from conquest by erosion,
headlights scour the highway
enroute to an ending
trust too, erodes.

Years, hence,
when I am smooth as sea glass on your beach
the coastal waterways will conspire
to erase these memories.

The Moon Gaslights the Sun

In my dream we are in a canoe
I am at bow, you stern, steering.
That was not how it really was:
I steered, you snookered me
to ignore my role,
feel insignificant.

That same dream, in a car
I passenger, you driver - not accurate,
I was the worker,
I maker, you taker.

The moon,
as you told it me,
illumines our life,
provides plants the power to thrive,
ends the working day with its ebbing rays,
steers the canoe,
drives the car,
all fakery, illusion and spell-casting.

In my dream your moon
dwarfs the all-powerful sun,
convinced of its helplessness,
my sun needed decades to assume
its position in the sky with confidence,
jettison lunar intrusion.

I am my sun
ascendant,
radiating beams,
defying dreams,
upholding our world
with my welcoming warmth

Sidney

The birth injury that hatched him
from aged seeds
nearest brother,
one score years older,
left my dad quite an only child,
home with past-it parents.

To whom could *he* look for love?

With obvious pride
he reveals to me:
My mom drove a big car.
Maybe a Packard in an ancient photo.
Alls he says about Anna.

What this means for him
escapes me.
Her stony face glares out
from the monochrome.

What I remember
now he's long gone:
air whizzes past my young head
as effortlessly he lifts
my tender frame
to a perch on his swole shoulder,
plunked close by his ear.
I never happier or safer.

His early deafness
from pop's repeated head blows
to a child's friable skull.

What I remember:
He offers to be lobotomized
to keep my mom happy.
Later,
he phones me from the asylum,
I'm being held prisoner on a ship.
Help me.
Then tied to his bed,
fed Thorazine.

What I remember:
I try to rescue him,
but his ship departs early.
He dies young.

I open the casket
to kiss his dry lips.
Wondering

to whom did *he* look for love?

Skate Story

About twenty of us
of various sizes, ages,
and roller-skating ability
glide effortlessly around
the Edison ellipse.

My right skate overtakes its mate
and the reverse.
"Thriller" blares over the speakers:
Under the moonlight
you see a sight
that almost stops your heart.

Tip one toe-stop for slowdown,
at my speed,
a lesson unlearned.

Off-balance,
I grab the railing,
crouch to avoid
the rapidly approaching skaters,
mostly children,
clattering past me
on the polished floor

and
    down
        I
            go.

Several children collect
around me
iron filings on a magnet.

I overcome by tears and nausea,
my shoulder aligns
with my cheek.

My thirteen-year-old
yanks off my skate,
seven-year-old
tugs unsuccessfully at my other foot.

Two adult skaters announce:
I'm an orthopedist;
he's an orthopedic surgeon.
I shiver a grateful sigh at my impending rescue.

From the shadows
the orthopedist offers: *Yup, dislocated. Get to a*
hospital.
His companion: *We can't touch you,*
blends gracefully
with the anonymous skaters scrambling around me.

Suddenly, my ex appears: *I have these kids.*
Good luck,
leaves me one-handed
to drive to the hospital
where the errant shoulder
w-o-b-b-l-e-s into place.

With a painkiller,
sling and referral chit,
no one asks why only one skate.

Salt of the Earth

Delicate as the rock of Gibraltar
and prettier
Aunt Connie, my model for mothering,
her five kids and a wide palette
of nieces, nephews and
unrelated hangers-on,
asleep on the porch divan,
crashed on the leaky beanbag furniture,
or in wee hours hunched over
the refrigerator,
prospecting for remnants of her legendary chili,
pickle relish or stuffed cabbage, golabki.

This assortment crept in
through the never-locked front door
or human-sized hole in the porch screen
always welcome to stay,
as long as they wished, or needed to.

She listened to
a juvenile's domestic issues,
shook her head, murmured, *Aw*
steeped tea leaves for them,
smeared tub margarine
on white toast, cut off the crusts.

There were DUIs
she drove to work, school or court.
No pushover,
she got her way
without you knowing how:
you lived right,
or better, for knowing her.

Famously generous, with the occasional
fiver slipped into a jean jacket,
she testified for a parent's
visitation or child custody rights,
met a school counselor
patiently explained that,
although called *Aunt*,
she was not an actual relative.

They nearly lost the house
for $30 taxes;
the community paid the overdue without asking.

Untrained in art,
with talent and a good eye,
her favorite times,
wielding easel and brush,
were painting from nature
at the cul-de sac,
to be hung at the diner.

She was in favor of marriage, children and family,
baked a sheet cake for my wedding
with homemade icing, cheery inscriptions,
pastel sugar flowers.

Her undivided, boundless love
for the luckless or fallen-on-bad-circumstances,
prevented them from making the wrong choice.

I never knew what she needed,
never asked,
as her love nourished me like none previous.

Gasp

The atmosphere and I commune
via two bellows in my chest;
their handy, teeny, air sacs
cash in oxygen,
cash out carbon dioxide,
an exchange beneficial,
universal even.

Plants use pores, stomata,
to pull off this transaction.
On earth, early critters,
before ears could hear,
used lungs to "get wind of"
sound pressures.

Now that the pulmonary function
test eludes me,
and a 5k looms less likely than before,
it is with increased respect and humility
that I tote around these chambers
resident in my chest
that sometimes, like now,
require a chemical nudge
to correctly perform.

The regular,
in-and-out basal rhythm
underscoring all else
never again will
be taken for granted
by this grateful breather.

My New Modern, Or Herbilly Elegy

Stove burners all light
don't need to drag dishwasher to faucet
can leave washing machine on, no flood
no more three flights' climb with groceries

outside lock works
plenty room to park
no rent raises
afford dental
don't need quarters for dryer
or get bedsheets stolen

more than minimum balance banked
credit not maxed
dependent-free
can shop Trader Joe's, but won't
don't have to share clothesline/garbage bins
with slobs next door

no broken elevators,
junkies on stoop,
vicious Dobermans,
or opera singers doing glottal stops
as neighbors

pension plan vested
made car payment
working doors and heater
hole-free upholstery
car passed inspection, praise the Lord
Children set in own lives
health okay good colleges
All's good

Unbooked, a Year Without Reading

The past year I spent lonely and unread.
No plays on scheming royalty,
matched couplets or biography,
magazines, travelogues, or mysteries,
newspapers or recipes.

My sightless eye charted the passage of time
making it patent and clear this constant reader
has vacated the premises once held so dear.

Blank pages in unopened journals
soullessly banked on shelves
not for me this day or year
as between the covers of the bed I lie.

This readerless year, static and blunt-edged,
saw me climbing a swaying ladder of syllables
reflected in a dim looking glass.

Pages smoother than satin in the past gave succor
and better days or years beckoned this reader
to yield to discovery.

A year in passing
lonely and unread
but in a moment the volume delivers
stoking the furnace of my comprehension.

Lining the passage of time with words
I encounter myself in the spaces and indents.
See me parked in the margins,
dust jackets deliver content to my heavy hands

I commemorate the year I dwelled bookless,
savor the sounds of the text
find empathy in dialogue.
Words soar like birds in migration,
banishing darkness from shut pages/unhandled
volumes.

About the Author

Roberta Batorsky is a biology teacher and freelance science writer. Her poetry reflects her interest in people, their lived experiences and science. She writes with empathy, knowledge, and humor. Her work has appeared in Heron Clan, Fine Lines, NJ Bards, Delaware Valley Poets, and other collections. This is her first book.

She lives in NJ with her husband and has 2 children and 2 grandchildren.

Her Instagram account is Robertabatorsky_poetry@instagram.com

www.ingramcontent.com/pod-product-compliance
Lightning Source LLC
Chambersburg PA
CBHW020412150626
46554CB00013B/744